SOCIAL STUDIES EXPLORER

It's Cool to Learn About the United States

NORTHEAST

➥ by Vicky Franchino

CHERRY LAKE PUBLISHING • ANN ARBOR, MICHIGAN

CHERRY LAKE Publishing

Published in the United States of America
by Cherry Lake Publishing
Ann Arbor, Michigan
www.cherrylakepublishing.com

Content Adviser: James Wolfinger, PhD, Associate Professor,
History and Teacher Education, DePaul University, Chicago, Illinois

Book design: The Design Lab

Photo credits: Cover and page 1, ©iStockphoto.com/messenjah,
©iStockphoto.com/KenWiedemann, ©iStockphoto.com/FernandoAH,
©iStockphoto.com/Ron_Thomas; page 4, ©Paul Lemke/Dreamstime.com;
page 5 and page 38, ©Songquan Deng/Dreamstime.com; page 6 and
page 39, ©Snehitdesign/Dreamstime.com; page 7a, ©iStockphoto.com/
Paul Tessier; page 7b, ©iStockphoto.com/Jerry Klavans; page 8, ©Marcio
Silva/Dreamstime.com; page 9, ???; page 10, ©janr34/Shutterstock,
Inc.; page 11, ©Suchan/Shutterstock, Inc.; page 13, ©Jeffrey M. Frank/
Shutterstock, Inc.; page 14, ©iStockphoto.com/HultonArchive; page 16,
©Paula Stephens/Dreamstime.com; page 17, ©Joshua Daniels/Dreamstime.
com; page 18, ©iStockphoto.com/Willowpix; page 20, ©Gina Sanders/
Shutterstock, Inc.; page 21, ©Donald Swartz/Dreamstime.com; page 22,
©Media Bakery/VisionsofAmerica/Joe Sohm; page 23, ©Gale Verhague/
Dreamstime.com; page 24, ©World History Archive/Alamy; page 25,
©iofoto/Shutterstock, Inc.; page 27, ©Kenk/Dreamstime.com; page 28,
©Julia Freeman-woolpert/Dreamstime.com; page 29, ©Media Bakery/
Jim Pickerell; page 30, ©Paul Hakimata/Dreamstime.com; page 31,
©Stephen Orsillo/Dreamstime.com; page 32, ©John Alphonse/Dreamstime.
com; page 33, ©Jiawangkun/Dreamstime.com; page 34, ©R. M. Hayman/
Dreamstime.com; page 36, ©Stuart Monk/Shutterstock, Inc.; page 37, ©Joy
Brown/Shutterstock, Inc.; page 40, ©Herbert Quick/Dreamstime.com; page
41, ©Karenfoleyphotography/Dreamstime.com; page 43, ©Markstout/
Dreamstime.com

Library of Congress Cataloging-in-Publication Data
Franchino, Vicky.
  It's cool to learn about the United States: Northeast/by Vicky
Franchino.
     p. cm.—(Social studies explorer)
  Includes bibliographical references and index.
  ISBN-13: 978-1-61080-180-5 (lib. bdg.)
  ISBN-13: 978-1-61080-305-2 (pbk.)
  1. Northeastern States—Juvenile literature. I. Title. II. Title: Northeast.
III. Series.
  F4.3.F73 2011
  974—dc22   2011003647

Cherry Lake Publishing would like to acknowledge the work
of The Partnership for 21st Century Skills. Please visit
www.21stcenturyskills.org for more information.

Printed in the United States of America
Corporate Graphics Inc.
July 2013
CLFA09

NORTHEAST

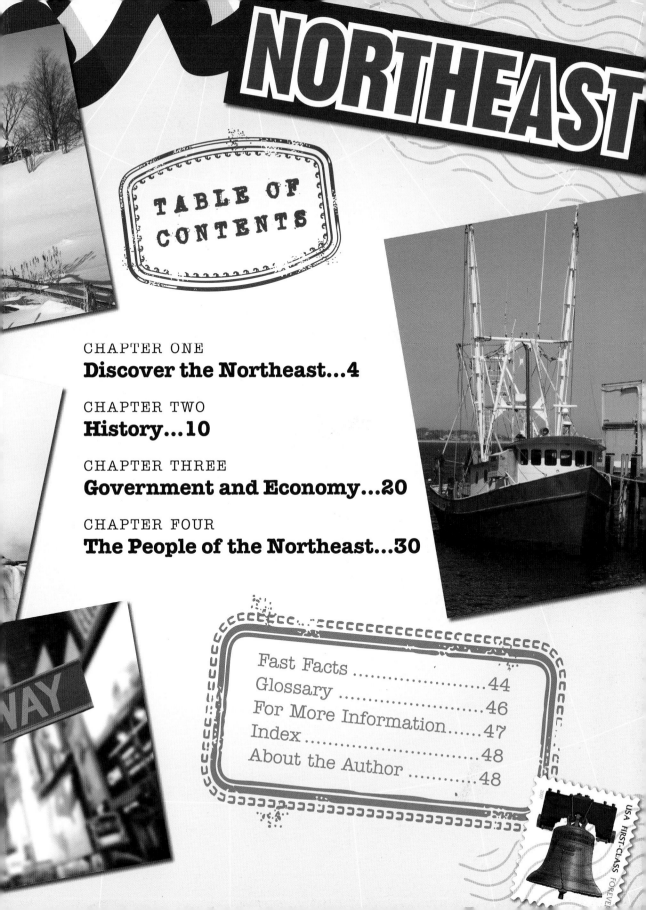

TABLE OF CONTENTS

CHAPTER ONE

DISCOVER THE NORTHEAST

☛ Cape Neddick, Maine, sits on the shore of the Atlantic Ocean.

You might find it hard to describe the northeastern part of the United States in a few words. It is a place where you can find the country's biggest city and some of its smallest towns. It is an area that has mountains,

beaches, and lakes, plus many kinds of animals and plants. The Northeast has shaped our country's past, and it will play an important part in creating our future. There are 11 states that are considered part of the Northeast: Connecticut, Delaware, Maine, Maryland, Massachusetts, New Hampshire, New Jersey, New York, Pennsylvania, Rhode Island, and Vermont.

◆ New York City's Times Square is always a busy place.

➤ A speedboat makes its way down the wide Allegheny River which runs through New York and Pennsylvania.

THE LOOK OF THE LAND

The Northeast is a place of great natural beauty. If you traveled throughout the Northeast, you would find many kinds of **topography**. Some areas would be flat, and others would be hilly or even mountainous. You would also find many beautiful lakes and rivers. Glaciers were the cause of this varied landscape. These giant mountains of ice last covered the earth about 10,000 years ago. As glaciers slowly traveled throughout the Northeast, they left behind valleys, mountains, and flat plains.

Much of the land in the Northeast is covered with forests. There has been an active lumber industry in the Northeast for hundreds of years, but more than half of the land is still covered with trees. Visitors come from all over the world to see these beautiful forests. Fall visits are especially popular because that is the time of year when **deciduous** trees, such as maple, oak, and beech, change color.

Animals found in the Northeast

The Northeast is home to many types of wildlife. You might not be surprised to learn that you can find black bears, deer, squirrels, raccoons, and rabbits. But did you know that you can also see more exotic animals? Visit New Hampshire and you'll find moose and the world's largest mammal, the whale. You might even spot a dolphin, a creature you would not expect to see so far north.

WEATHER AND CLIMATE

Some northeastern states have somewhat extreme weather. Others have milder temperatures and lower amounts of rain and snow. Vermont usually receives more than 6 feet (1.8 meters) of snow each year, while Delaware can get less than 2 feet (0.61 m) each year. In summer months, Maryland tends to be hot and humid, while Maine enjoys cooler temperatures. Some northeastern areas, like Long Island, New York, frequently have hurricane warnings, although they are uncommon in Pennsylvania.

ACTIVITY

STATE CAPITALS

Trace or make a copy of this map, and fill in the names of the 11 northeastern states and their capitals. You might need to do a little investigating to find out which city pairs up with its correct match!

STOP
Don't write in this book!

STATES:
Connecticut
Delaware
Maine
Maryland
Massachusetts
New Hampshire
New Jersey
New York
Pennsylvania
Rhode Island
Vermont

CAPITALS:
Harrisburg
Augusta
Montpelier
Boston
Hartford
Albany
Dover
Providence
Concord
Annapolis
Trenton

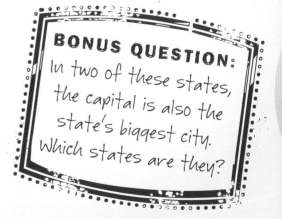

BONUS QUESTION:
In two of these states, the capital is also the state's biggest city. Which states are they?

Answer: Massachusetts and Rhode Island

CHAPTER TWO

HISTORY

➥ Animal skins could be used for clothing or in trade.

Scientists believe that people first lived in the Northeast more than 10,000 years ago. We do not know much about the earliest people who lived there. But we do know a lot about the Native Americans living there when the first European explorers arrived.

EARLY INHABITANTS

Native Americans living in the Northeast included Lenni-Lenape, Nanticoke, Abenaki, and Mahicans. Each group had its own culture and tradition, but they all knew how to survive the harsh conditions of the Northeast. The Native Americans knew how to grow crops and how to hunt wild animals for food. They built homes out of the trees and plants they found in the forests. Sadly, the colonists from Europe brought diseases with them that killed countless Native Americans. Many Native Americans also were forced to leave their lands as the colonists aggressively pushed west.

⏵ Many Native Americans in the Northeast lived in wigwams.

WHO COLONIZED THE NORTHEAST?

Although nine of the northeastern states eventually became English **colonies**, some were first settled by other European countries. Some of these settlements were little more than a fort and a trading post, but others were larger.

STATE	FIRST EUROPEAN SETTLEMENT
Connecticut	Dutch
Delaware*	Dutch and Swedish
Maine	French
Maryland	English
Massachusetts	English
New Hampshire	English
New Jersey*	Dutch and Swedish
New York	Dutch
Pennsylvania*	Dutch and Swedish
Rhode Island	English
Vermont	French

*Both the Dutch and Swedes had some type of settlement in this state and fought for control of the area.

THE BIRTH OF A NATION

England fought an expensive war against the French for control of the Northeast, known as the French and Indian War, or the Seven Years' War (1754–1763). England won the conflict, but it had borrowed large sums of money to fight the French. To pay back its large **debt**, England imposed taxes on the colonists to raise money. Many of the colonists were angered because they did not have representation in Parliament, England's legislature, which was approving the taxes. The anger on both sides soon flared into bitter conflict.

◆ Fort Ticonderoga in New York was built by the French in the 1750s.

◆ Washington and his troops crossing the Delaware River is one of the most famous events of the American Revolution.

In 1775, fighting broke out between American colonists and English soldiers in the Massachusetts cities of Lexington and Concord. On July 4, 1776, the colonies announced their freedom from England by signing the Declaration of Independence. Yet it took the loss of many lives during the American Revolutionary War (1775–1783) before the colonies could establish their own nation. In 1787, representatives from most of the new states met in Philadelphia to create the U.S. **Constitution**.

A NEW COUNTRY

The Northeast states were among the first to be admitted to the United States. They officially achieved statehood on the following dates.

STATE	DATE OF STATEHOOD	STATE NUMBER
Delaware	December 7, 1787	1st
Pennsylvania	December 12, 1787	2nd
New Jersey	December 18, 1787	3rd
Connecticut	January 9, 1788	5th
Massachusetts	February 6, 1788	6th
Maryland	April 28, 1788	7th
New Hampshire	June 21, 1788	9th
New York	July 26, 1788	11th
Rhode Island	May 29, 1790	13th
Vermont	March 4, 1791	14th
Maine	March 15, 1820	23rd

BITTER DIVISION

The 1800s were a time of growth in the Northeast. The **Industrial Revolution** had begun, and goods were being made with machines, rather than by hand. People and goods were able to travel quickly from city to city as the system of railroads grew. Railroad construction provided jobs for many people. While the northeastern states began to rely on machines, the southern states continued to use **slaves** to run their farms and industries.

◆ Factories like this one were built in the Northeast during the 1800s.

◆ People with an interest in Civil War history gather to reenact battles.

Southern states **seceded** from the Union after decades of bitter debate between Southern and Northern states. They formed the Confederate States of America. Eventually, the bad feelings led to the American Civil War (1861–1865). All of the states in the Northeast remained part of the Union during the Civil War. Not everyone in the region, however, agreed with his or her state's official decision to remain. In Maryland and Delaware some people fought for the Union, or the North, and some fought for the Confederacy, or the South.

Two of the most famous Civil War battles took place in the Northeast. These were the Battle of Antietam in Maryland in 1862 and the Battle of Gettysburg in Pennsylvania in 1863. By the end of the war, more than 600,000 soldiers had died. Slavery was abolished with the 13th **Amendment** to the Constitution just before the war ended. The divided nation began the hard work of joining together again.

The battlefield at Gettysburg has been a national park since 1895.

ACTIVITY

WHO AM I?

The Northeast has been home to many important people. See if you can match the person with his or her accomplishment.

PERSON	ACCOMPLISHMENT
1. Harriet Beecher Stowe	a. Member of Patuxet peoples; helped Pilgrims at Plymouth colony; from Massachusetts area
2. Joe Biden	b. U.S. astronaut who walked on the moon; from New Jersey
3. E. B. White	c. Scientist who discovered the vaccine for polio; from New York
4. Thurgood Marshall	d. First African American justice on U.S. Supreme Court; from Delaware
5. Squanto	e. Actor and comedian; from Pennsylvania
6. Nathan Hale	f. Escaped Nazis in Austria and story was told in *The Sound of Music*; from Vermont
7. Edwin "Buzz" Aldrin	g. Wrote *Uncle Tom's Cabin*; from Connecticut
8. Jonas Salk	h. Author of *Charlotte's Web*; from Maine
9. Bill Cosby	i. Famous artist who painted picture of George Washington that appears on $1 bill; from Rhode Island
10. Gilbert Stuart	j. U.S. senator and vice president to the first African American president; from Delaware
11. Von Trapp family	k. American patriot during Revolutionary War; from New Hampshire

Answers: 1-g; 2-j; 3-h; 4-d; 5-a; 6-k; 7-b; 8-c; 9-e; 10-i; 11-f.

STOP
Don't write in this book!

CHAPTER THREE

GOVERNMENT AND ECONOMY

➥ The Statue of Liberty was one of the first sights to greet immigrants when they arrived in New York City by ship.

Many European **immigrants** came to the Northeast in the years after the Civil War. They wanted to find work in the new factories that had opened. The working and

living conditions in their new nation were often harsh. But that did not prevent hundreds of thousands of immigrants from making the long journey to start new lives in the United States. They saw America as a place of opportunity for themselves and their families.

More than 12 million immigrants entered the United States at Ellis Island from 1892 to 1954. Some parts of the island are in New York and others are in New Jersey. Upon arriving at Ellis Island, each immigrant had his or her documents checked and approved. Each new arrival also had to pass a physical examination. Today, Ellis Island is a museum owned by the U.S. government.

WATERWAYS

Water played an important role in the success of the northeastern states. New York's natural harbor was an excellent place for ships to bring goods into and out of the country. The Erie Canal connected the Great Lakes with the Atlantic Ocean and made it possible to ship goods around the United States and to Europe. The Delaware and Connecticut Rivers provided easy ways to send goods throughout the area. Water was also a

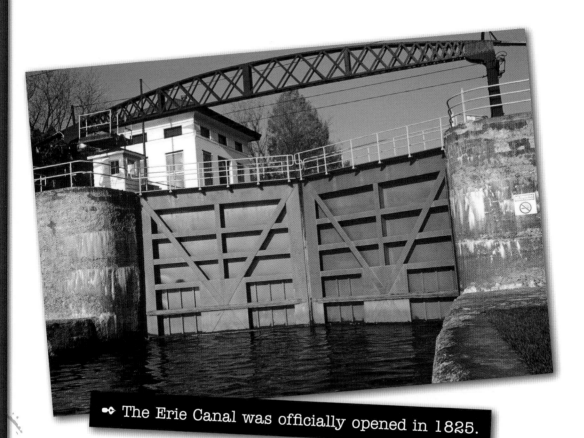

➥ The Erie Canal was officially opened in 1825.

•❖ Sap from maple trees is collected in buckets as a first step in making maple syrup.

source of power. It ran the mills that produced food, paper, and textiles.

Fishing provided a livelihood for thousands of workers throughout the Northeast, and shipbuilding was a common industry. Farming was important to the Northeast in the early years. Over time, however, fewer people earned their living from farming. Agriculture still plays an important role in the region's economy. Dairy products, apples, maple sugar, and poultry are produced in much of the Northeast.

◆ Unemployed men wait in line for a meal during the Great Depression.

AN INDUSTRIAL BOOM

The factories of the Northeast provided ships, weapons, chemicals, steel, and canned food to U.S. troops during World War I (1914–1918). Many of these factories closed during the Great Depression (1929–1940) putting a lot of people out of work.

When World War II (1939–1945) began, the factories of the Northeast again played an important role in

providing the tools and equipment the military needed. Since World War II, there have been many changes in how the people of the Northeast earn a living. Many factories have closed and moved to other countries where labor is cheaper. Today more people throughout the Northeast work in service industries. People in service industries include doctors, teachers, police officers, and others who serve the public or other industries.

⊷ Many people in the Northeast work in service industry jobs, such as teaching.

WHAT KINDS OF JOBS DO PEOPLE HAVE IN PENNSYLVANIA?

Pie charts are a good way to compare things. For this activity, use a pie chart to show the different types of jobs that people have in the state of Pennsylvania. Trace a large circle on a piece of paper. Then divide the circle into pieces, just as if you were dividing a pie.

Use the numbers below to decide how to divide your pie.

INDUSTRY	PERCENTAGE OF WORKERS IN THIS INDUSTRY
Education and health services	20%
Trade, transportation, and retail	19%
Goods producing (mining, logging, construction, manufacturing)	14%
Leisure, hospitality, and other services	13%
Government	13%
Professional business services	12%
Information and financial services	6%

Source: Center for Workforce Information and Analysis (CWIA), November 2010. Percentages do not add up to 100 because of rounding.

THE STRUCTURE OF GOVERNMENT

Each of the 11 states in the Northeast has a government structure that is similar to the U.S. government. As in the **federal** government, there are three branches: executive, legislative, and judicial. Having three different groups helps to make sure that one branch is unable to take control of the government.

↝ The New Jersey legislature meets in the State House in the state capital of Trenton.

The governor is the head of the executive branch. The voters in the state elect the governor. In most states, the governor serves a 4-year term, but in New Hampshire and Vermont, the term is only 2 years. In New Hampshire, the governor can serve only one time, but there is no limit in Vermont.

The legislative branch makes the laws. Typically, there is a senate and a house of representatives. There

◆ Jeanne Shaheen served as the first woman elected governor of New Hampshire before running for the U.S. Senate.

•→ The judicial branch is in charge of criminal and other legal trials.

are a certain number of senators from each of the counties in the state. The number of representatives depends on the population of the county.

The judicial branch deals with legal issues. It helps to interpret the laws that the legislative branch passes. The judicial branch must often decide if the laws follow the state's constitution.

CHAPTER FOUR

THE PEOPLE OF THE NORTHEAST

�«➙ People who emigrate from the same country often settle near one another in neighborhoods such as New York City's Chinatown.

In America's early years, most people immigrated to the United States from European countries. Today, you can find immigrants from nearly every country in the world. Some of the populations of the northeastern states are very **diverse**, while others are not.

SMALL STATES, LARGE STATES

The smaller states, such as New Hampshire, Maine, and Vermont, have populations that are more than 90 percent Caucasian. The states with larger populations, such as New York, Pennsylvania, and New Jersey, have a greater variety of people. In New York, African Americans and Hispanics each make up 17 percent of the population, and the Asian population is 7 percent of the total. The highest percentage of African Americans

➥ Large cities in other northeastern states, such as Boston, Massachusetts, also have diverse populations.

in the Northeast is in Maryland, where 29 percent of the population is black.

SIGHTS TO SEE, THINGS TO DO

The cities in the far northeastern states of Maine, Vermont, and New Hampshire are generally small. Here you'll find plenty of outdoor activities and old-fashioned celebrations. Maine makes the most of the winter months with a toboggan championship. It celebrates its brief

➥ St. Rocco's Bazaar, also called St. Peter's Italian Street Festival, takes place every summer in Portland, Maine.

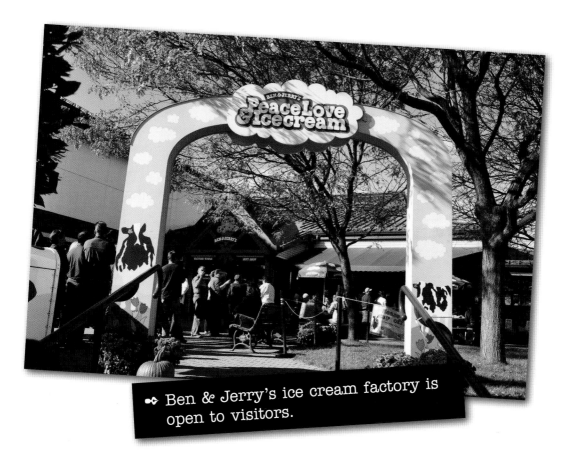

↦ Ben & Jerry's ice cream factory is open to visitors.

summer with a lobster festival and other oceanside activities. Vermont offers winter carnivals, maple sugar festivals, and tours of the Ben and Jerry's ice cream factory. Go to New Hampshire for carnivals that celebrate all the fun things you can do with ice and snow. You can also visit seafood festivals and beautiful state parks while you are there. Whether you like big cities or the slower pace of the countryside, Massachusetts has a lot

*◦ Sailing is a popular sport in Cape Cod.

to do. In the capital city of Boston, you can check out historical sights such as Paul Revere's house and the Boston Tea Party Ships and Museum. You can also go to the John F. Kennedy Presidential Library and Museum. Visit the beautiful Berkshire Mountains for hiking or skiing. Head to Cape Cod where you can sail, swim, or visit art galleries and shops.

WHAT DO THEY LIKE TO EAT IN . . .

In America's melting-pot culture, it is easy to find food from all over the world, no matter where you travel. But there are still some foods that are special to a geographic area.

STATE	POPULAR FOOD
Connecticut	No Thanksgiving is complete without cranberries.
Delaware	Their famous blue crabs make delicious crab cakes.
Maine	Buy a lobster right off a fishing boat!
Maryland	Smith Island Cake is a delicious treat that has up to 10 layers.
Massachusetts	Old-fashioned Boston baked beans are a state favorite.
New Hampshire	Apple cider, apple pies, and apple crisp!
New Jersey	Blueberries are the official state fruit.
New York	Hot dogs, bagels, and pizza are New York favorites.
Pennsylvania	Philly cheesesteak sandwiches combine cheese and thinly sliced beef.
Rhode Island	If you like deep-fried dough covered with sugar, you'll like doughboys.
Vermont	Maple syrup is perfect for pancakes.

Connecticut is a great state to visit if you like the beach. It also has plenty of unusual museums. Check out The New England Carousel Museum in Bristol if you are a merry-go-round fan. If speed is more your thing, visit the New England Air Museum or the Stafford Motor Speedway.

Rhode Island is the country's smallest state, but it offers plenty of big fun. Learn more about lighthouses,

↦ Lighthouses can be seen along many Connecticut beaches.

◆ Many towns and cities, such as Providence, Rhode Island, have historic districts filled with small shops.

sailboats, art, and farms at one of the state's many museums. Visit beaches, wildlife refuges, and zoos. Maybe you can even catch the ghost at Rhode Island's Sprague Mansion!

There are so many things to do in the state of New York that it could be very hard to pick the best ones. If you like big cities, there is no better place than the Big Apple, New York City. It is the country's largest city

➻ The Bethesda Fountain is only one of many places to gather in New York's Central Park.

and is home to theaters, museums and Central Park. It also offers some of the world's best shopping and people watching. New York State is also where you will find Niagara Falls, one of the world's most impressive water-falls. Check out the Adirondacks, especially in the fall. It's a beautiful mountain range in the northeastern part of the state.

Many people think that New Jersey only has factories and big cities. They might be surprised to

learn it has many beautiful parks and beaches. It also has museums, aquariums, and festivals that celebrate everything from blueberries to polkas.

Like all of the states in the Northeast, Pennsylvania is home to both natural beauty and historical treasures. You will not want to miss this state's Grand Canyon at Pine Creek Gorge. Visit the beautiful Allegheny National Forest to see some of the Northeast's most breathtaking natural scenery.

Pennsylvania's Allegheny National Forest bursts into color during the fall.

Head to Philadelphia if history is your thing. There you can visit the places where George Washington, John Adams, Thomas Jefferson, and Benjamin Franklin helped shape a new country.

Delaware is a small state with a lot to offer. It is home to historical buildings, museums, and cultural events such as plays and ballets. It also offers action-packed activities such as NASCAR racing.

↔ Visitors can see historic planes at the Air Mobility Command Museum in Dover, Delaware.